Heroin
Addicts

How to Help a Heroin Addict
Before It's Too Late

~ A Guide to Understanding Heroin Addiction ~

by Anne C. Mapehrson

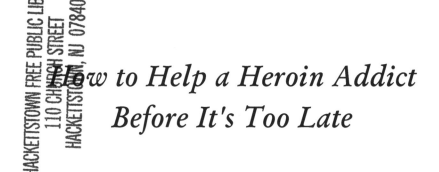

Donated
by

Hackettstown
Alliance for
Drug Prevention

— It takes a community —

Table of Contents

Introduction..1

Chapter 1: Understanding Heroin Addiction...................7

Chapter 2: Recognizing Heroin Paraphernalia...............13

Chapter 3: Signs and Symptoms of Heroin Abuse........17

Chapter 4: Side Effects of Heroin....................................23

Chapter 5: Treatment Options for Heroin Addiction ..29

Chapter 6: Recovering from Heroin Addiction.............39

Conclusion 43

Introduction

How to help a heroin addict before it is too late is a frightening title, but it is a gentler way of saying... before they die. That is a very real possibility of what may happen if they do not recognize and overcome their addiction.

You have a heroin addict in the family, and you are worried that if you do not do something to help him/her, you will live to regret it. We are here to tell you what you can do to help.

Heroin addiction is quite possibly the worst of all drug addictions. The road to recovery is normally a very long and torturous one for not only the user but also the caregivers and the people who live with the addict; friends (if any) and family.

It may be a long journey, but that does not mean it's an insurmountable one. With the right kind of treatment and care, it is possible to recover from heroin addiction and overcome the dependency altogether, but you need to be informed about how to achieve this as well as what to expect along the way.

This book will help answer some of the more urgent questions you may be asking. For example, why do heroin users develop such a high dependency on the drug? What are the signs of heroin addiction? What are the different types of treatment that may be used to help a recovering addict? What are some of the withdrawal symptoms to look out for?

That a heroin junkie will seldom admit to their addiction doesn't make things any easier. In fact, it makes everything so hard, trying to help someone who thinks they do not need any help, except maybe with their next shot.

It is not the time to play blame games with the victim. It is time to help them before they become just another statistic. When it comes to heroin addiction, the situation is not about what started it, but it is about their being a victim of a drug that has the power to cuff an individual even more strongly than steel manacles. Not many addicts can overcome this addiction on their own. It will take a lot of love, support, and care from you. But how do you get started? This book will answer that.

4

Chapter 1: Understanding Heroin Addiction

Before going to war, every good warrior knows the essence of knowing their enemy and understands the best strategies to employ and deploy if you wish to win. The same concept applies to helping a loved one overcome heroin addiction.

How much do you really know about this drug?

What is Heroin?

Scientifically known as diacetylmorphine, heroin is a derivative of morphine, which is produced from opium. If you could just see the poppy plantations splashed across the fields in southern Asia, you would find it difficult to believe that such a small, beautiful flower could give rise to the monstrosity that is heroin. But the poppy is not a hazardous drug until it is processed and enters the body.

Currently, research shows that heroin is almost three times more potent than morphine and it is highly addictive.

Perhaps one reason why heroin often escapes notice is because it comes in various forms. Pure heroin is a white powder and has a bitter taste. On the streets, you would rarely find it being sold in its pure form. It is normally "cut" with other drugs and substances such as sugar, powdered milk, starch, or quinine. Some even cut it with poisons such as strychnine just so they can get a more aggressive "rush".

"Black tar" is a variation of heroin that comes in a darker color – anywhere from dark brown to black. This variety is not in powder form. It may be sticky like tar or even hard like coal.

Modes of Administration

The most popular way of taking heroin is by injecting it either into a muscle (whereby effects are felt after 5 to 8 minutes) or directly into the vein (in which case effects are felt after 7 to 8 seconds). However, this is not the only way in which the drug may enter one's system. It may also be sniffed, smoked, ingested orally or even used as a suppository. Whichever method is used, it still has the ability to be addictive.

The different methods of taking it will only have an impact on the "rush" experienced in terms of its intensity and how long it takes to kick in.

When ingested orally, there is no "rush" experienced. When sniffed or smoked, it will give rise to a rush, but it will not be as intense as that experienced when the drug is taken in by IV injection. Taking the drug in suppository form is common among the hard-core addicts; as it tends to have very intense euphoric effects.

Using IV injections is the method most commonly used and yet it is the one method that may have the greatest repercussions such as higher risk of infections or transmitted diseases when syringes are shared, great risk of directly damaging the veins, and the highest chance of overdosing.

Furthermore, when heroin is taken by injection or by smoking – since it actually bypasses the liver as opposed to the case with oral ingestion, it does not undergo the liver metabolism thus causing it to pose a higher risk to one's body and internal organs.

Addictive Properties of Heroin

What happens when you take in heroin? What about it makes the user develop such a high dependency on the drug in such a relatively short period of time?

When heroin enters the body, it begins by looking for receptors commonly found scattered in the brain and even in the intestinal tract. The heroin molecules will attach themselves to these receptors and, as expected, this will result in a cascade of chemical reactions.

Heroin use displays euphoric, anxiolytic, and analgesic central nervous system properties, so the chemical reactions produced will involve the pleasure centers of the brain.

Acting under the influence of heroin, the brain will tend to release large amounts of dopamine – the chemical associated with feelings of pleasure, such as when you are about to open a gift or when you are looking forward to indulging in a mouth-watering meal, only that when heroin is involved, this feeling will be exaggerated and prolonged. Novice users will have a high lasting even up to 6 hours.

This state of euphoria may be a happy experience for the user but the brain will not share the same sentiment. In a bid to "protect" itself, the brain adjusts its response to pleasure signals and builds a "tolerance" to the same dosage. What this means is that the next time you take the same dose, it will lead to a lesser high. The user will have to increase the dosage so that he/she may experience the initial original high. Again, this is taken into the body and, once more, the brain makes adjustments to its response.

This cycle of buildup of tolerance followed by an increase in dosage will go on until it reaches a point whereby the brain has made so many adjustments that it simply cannot function normally without the heroin. This is why most people rarely just "dabble" when it comes to heroin. With the first hit you just might very likely end up getting hooked on this drug.

Chapter 2: Recognizing Heroin Paraphernalia

Of course, before you can begin administering treatment to a heroin addict, you have to be sure that they are indeed abusing the drug. In the absence of all other proof, one way to tell is if you happen to come across paraphernalia commonly associated with heroin. These are basically the 'tools' used in the preparation, injection, and consumption of heroin. Before moving on to more insidious stuff, let's start off with some seemingly harmless signs and work our way up to more obvious paraphernalia.

Are you starting to observe that more shoelaces or ties are going missing? These seemingly unrelated items are used to tie off the injection sites so that the constriction of blood flow would make the vein more visible, and thus easier to inject into.

If you notice small plastic bags with suspicious white powder or residue, it's always best to be rather more curious about the contents. A simple sniff and the tiniest of lick from a dabbed fingertip usually suffices to tell whether the contents are any of the usual suspects found around the house. If these tastes don't reveal its identity successfully, it's advisable to – without exception or delay – submit the bag for testing at a laboratory. It's always better to be wrong and red-faced about mistaking some sherbet for drugs, than to be right and negligent in one's actions.

If more and more small items such as straws, aluminum foil pieces, silver spoons and gum wrappers are turning up with burn marks, it's a pretty prominent red flag. These paraphernalia are commonly used to heat and liquefy the heroin powder before injecting it through a syringe. A similarly suspicious element is to have syringes and needles lying or hidden around, without any underlying medical conditions which would necessitate their storage around one's house, and regular use. A final sign is the presence of water pipes or other similar pipes for smoking heroin. These can easily be hidden around the house, and since the user isn't injecting him/herself, it leaves rather less physical evidence of the addiction on the addict's person – making it harder to detect or prove.

It sounds like quite a long shot to go snooping around looking for these items so perhaps the next section will help you better identify whether your loved one is abusing heroin. But even without further proof, if your parental instincts truly tell you that something is amiss, by all means snoop around.

Chapter 3: Signs and Symptoms of Heroin Abuse

Like most people addicted to any drug, heroin users will display a variety of signs and symptoms. These may be witnessed as soon as a couple of minutes after taking a hit, whereas other signs may still be visible even after years of heroin dependency.

Short Term Effects

The very first effects of heroin use are rather short term but may be seen immediately one takes a hit of the drug.

Out of these, the more obviously visible ones after an addict takes a "hit" of the drug are the "rush" or the euphoric surge which is experienced by the user. The addict is beset with feelings of joyful contentment and peace. At the same time, physiologically, the user may be seen to suffer from a rather warm flushing of the skin accompanied by dry mouth. A long, droopy and heavy quality seems to weigh down their limbs and their pupils often appear like "pinpoints" - constricted or unnaturally small. A certain shortness of breath is observed, along with a lowered ability to cough which often leads to a feeling of nausea, retching or vomiting if any outside substance is actively irritating the upper respiratory tract or the stomach lining.

Apart from the effects listed above, the last two prominently observable short term characteristics seen in a heroin user soon after their last dose is inexplicable drowsiness – especially if they've had a decent amount of sleep at night – and consistent itching of their skin. Like other opiates, heroin affects the action and amount of neurotransmitters and reduces the effective ability of the brain to perceive pain. After the initially enjoyable euphoric surge, the user will tend to experience observable highs and lows of hyperactivity followed by drowsiness. Disorientation may be another commonly seen symptom since the central nervous system is depressed when under the influence of heroin.

Behavioral Signs

The scariest part of drug abuse isn't that these drugs trigger physiological changes in body and brain chemistry upon long-term use, but rather that prolonged use also brings with it the typical behavior of an addict – maladaptive psychological responses to a dysfunctional situation which reinforces its own patterns and cycles. Basically, such long term abuse turns the mentality of a user into that of an addict – all of which is geared to make them sink deeper into the addiction.

As would be expected in cases of drug abuse, constant sleepiness or unexplained drowsiness is a rather common clue. The highs and lows of abuse keep them strung up within this cycle. What may also be observed is incoherent or slurred speech, and it may be noticed that this seems to become slightly more prominent as more time passes. A sheer negligence of personal hygiene or of cleanliness in the space around them is another long-term behavioral effect in drug users. This is partly caused by the lethargy of drug abuse, but also because of the massive drop in self-esteem observed in addicts – which can be determined by an increase in self-hating comments or an increased pessimism in the user.

In such cases, deception is more commonly seen. Since addicts rather strongly refuse a dose of reality – so much so that that's why they take psychoactive drugs – the usual triggers and accompaniments of deception are usual fare. Thus, addicts will inexplicably lie to cover up their actions, expenses, habits, etc. However, these lies will be accompanied by a loss in productivity and a severe lack of motivation, drive or enthusiasm – whether at school, work, etc. Theft and fiscal irresponsibility may also be observed since users need a steady supply of money to maintain the habit, and provide for the next "hit". Users will also tend to have a distant look in their eyes, and may avoid making direct eye contact.

Drug addicts often have a difficult time bonding with normal, healthy, well-adjusted peers and so prefer to isolate themselves more and more from their family and previous circles of friends while increasingly being seen in contact with friends with whom they have no logical reason to be socially aligning themselves. Essentially, they start hanging around and spending more time with other addicts rather than well-adjusted people. The behavioral changes, coupled with the low self-esteem, may also trigger feelings of resentment in the user towards his/her environment along with misplaced hostility and an attitude of blaming one's own predicaments on everything and everybody else around.

Lastly, and this one should stand out like an elephant in the middle of Times Square, addicts (especially those who use syringes) tend to develop rather strange dressing habits (long sleeves when it's insanely hot outside, etc.) in order to cover up the needle marks. If this sort of behavior is observed, don't be too quick to attribute it to teenage, or a dressing phase in style, etc. Check before you explain it away.

Physical Signs

As previously explained, the body reacts with every intake of heroin and so it will reach a point whereby the user will have completely developed a tolerance to heroin, making them dependent on the drug. When this happens, the physical signs of heroin abuse will become more distinct.

In cases of heroin dependence, a seemingly perpetually runny nose or an unending case of the "sniffles" is seen which isn't explained by the presence of any medical condition or allergies. This is often accompanied by a sudden and significant weight loss brought on by the drug abuse as well as several cuts, scabs and bruises on their skin because of the incessant itching caused by the drug abuse. The bruises and cuts may also get infected due to the negligence of personal hygiene. These infections may also be rather prominent on or around the scores of needle marks at injection sites – usually seen around the forearms close to the crook in the elbow, or between toes.

Heroin users also prominently have a rather distant gaze in their eyes. It has been said that heroin "steals the soul". Lastly, in women, drug abuse leads to amenorrhea – the suppression or complete absence of the normal menstrual flow.

Chapter 4: Side Effects of Heroin

In this chapter, you will see why it is very important to do something to save a heroin addict as soon as possible. Heroin can cause death, either directly, from an overdose, or indirectly, from the contraction of other diseases.

There are so many things that can go wrong when someone is a heroin addict. The truth is that unless something is done, it's unlikely for a person to live ten more years with the addiction. Sooner or later, it will most likely kill them.

Besides the disorienting physical symptoms of heroin addiction, long term use of heroin could also lead to quite a number of adverse effects on the user, among which include:

- It could potentially change how genes are activated in the brain, thus changing brain function not only of the user but also of the user's offspring.

- Increased risk of miscarriage (spontaneous abortion)

- Infection can very easily lead to the loss of a limb.

- There is an increased risk of overdosing as the user continues to build a tolerance to the drug.

- Stomach contents can be breathed into the lungs, thus causing choking, infection, or even death.

- Constant vomiting and diarrhea will not only cause dehydration but also imbalance the body's chemical make-up.

- The user could develop depression, leading to suicidal thoughts.

- Hepatitis C

- HIV and AIDS

- Toxic reactions to heroin impurities - some of the additives added to street heroin do not really dissolve into the body. As a result, they can lead to clogged blood vessels which will cause organ failure either in part or wholly.

- Collapsed veins

- Inflammation of the heart lining and valves (endocarditis)

- Pneumonia - resulting from the fact that the user will tend to neglect their personal hygiene and care, and also from the impact of heroin on the respiratory system).

- Heroin overdose

When heroin is taken by way of IV injection, it is much easier to overdose because it is being injected directly into the blood stream. Even an excess dose of just a couple of milligrams will be near fatal.

Some of the signs and symptoms of heroin overdose are:

- o Labored and shallow breathing
- o Muscle spasms
- o Hypotension
- o Convulsions
- o Coma
- o Death

Withdrawal Symptoms

Once the body has developed a dependency on heroin, the user may experience withdrawal effects even several hours after their last hit. Usually, the withdrawal effects are torturous for the addict and many will tend to inject another dose just so they may be relieved of the withdrawal effects.

When one is recovering, however, they may not have the luxury of taking hits to reduce the withdrawal symptoms. As a caregiver, what are some of the withdrawal effects that you should look out and be prepared for?

- Agitation
- Irritability
- Nausea
- Vomiting
- Anxiety
- Diarrhea
- Stomach cramps
- Trouble sleeping
- Fever or Chills
- Abnormal Sweating
- Dehydration
- Sinus congestion or runs
- Other allergy-like symptoms
- Body Fatigue
- Muscle aches and pains
- Dilated pupils
- Tearing of the eyes
- Yawning
- Strong drug cravings

In the most extreme cases the user may experience hallucinations or even suicidal thoughts. Be prepared for quite a gruesome sight because the user will actually suffer physically, and it will seem like they are being tormented. However, as a caregiver, you must be strong for the both of you if you want the treatment to succeed. It's always a good idea to work with a doctor during the recovery phase, and seek help you're your doctor immediately if any of the withdrawal symptoms appear life-threatening or simply unbearable.

Chapter 5: Treatment Options for Heroin Addiction

When it comes to treating heroin addiction, one may use either behavioral treatment or pharmacological treatment, although a combination of the two has been proven to be the most effective way to restore some level of normalcy to brain functions, as well as re-adjust the addict's behavior. Support groups should also be included in the addict's treatment program.

Heroin Detox

The first step to any heroin treatment regime should be detoxification. This is where the patient stops taking heroin and will begin to overcome his/her dependence on the drug. As much as this step is very important, it is also very dangerous and so it should be done with much care. This is where the real harm that heroin can do is witnessed, and you may be surprised that the person is your relative or friend.

When the body has developed a dependency on a substance, which in this case is the brain becoming dependent on heroin, depriving it of the drug could even be fatal. Many patients have at this stage reported various withdrawal symptoms mentioned in the previous chapter.

There are two types of heroin detox commonly used:

Natural detox

This is where the addict quits heroin cold turkey. They stop taking the drug completely and give the body time to re-adjust. Of course, this type of detox will also lead to some of the most brutal withdrawal symptoms, and the user is very likely to relapse.

In natural detox, you are going to help the addict quit heroin cold turkey. Yes, just like that, - wake up one morning and decide no more heroin. You think this is easy? Do not delude yourself. This is where the addict will fight the battle of and for their life. It will be very difficult to witness.

Stock up on water! This could be all you will need for starters if you are doing a natural detox. We all know that water helps flush toxins out of the system. In addition, since one of the withdrawal symptoms will include the loss of appetite, water will help him/her stay hydrated at least. As hydrated muscles can respond well to strain, water is going to help the body regulate the temperature. With water, one will respond better to treatment.

You will need a natural heroin detox plan

A heroin detox plan will keep you on track with helping your loved one overcome heroin addiction. You will need a plan that can be customized to meet the unique needs of the addict. Luckily, there are many standard heroin detox plans on the internet and elsewhere that can be customized to suit the needs of various patients. Getting a plan is one thing, but making sure that the patient adheres to the plan to the letter is another thing altogether.

Medical detox

Someone said that heroin withdrawal symptoms can be worse than flu symptoms, multiplied by 1000. Stopping the consumption of opium will be the hardest thing that you have ever done in your life, but even harder will be keeping the urges away.

Having less intense withdrawal symptoms, the medical detox uses methadone – a synthetic opiate. Gradually, the methadone dose issued gets smaller and smaller until the patient eventually overcomes their physical heroin addiction.

During this phase, gastric and muscular distress can be soothed using over-the-counter medications. There are many to choose from. However, it is best to select the most reputed one and follow the advice of an addiction specialist.

Counseling

Normally done together with detoxification, the main purpose of counseling is to get the patient through the torturous withdrawal symptoms. It is up to the caregiver to find a professional skilled in counseling to help the addict understand that the physical pain is only temporary and will soon end. You would be surprised by how much counseling assists in preventing relapses.

Counseling doesn't *just* help in distracting a user from the intense physical pain of withdrawal but allows them to delve deeper into their own psyche as well, in a controlled medical environment, so that they can better understand the origin and pattern of their addiction. This will be invaluable later on in helping to prevent relapses, especially if the patient can understand the mental triggers which cause them to reach out for drugs each time. If the drug abuse is a result of mental or emotional trauma, then counseling helps by highlighting said trauma and then working to help the patient heal from it.

As we discussed before, long-term drug abuse doesn't just come with a host of physiological or chemical changes, but brings with it a host of behavioral patterns as well – some of which are the self-esteem issues, hostility, pessimism and negativity seen in addicts. Counseling helps a patient psychologically rehabilitate so that they can start their journey towards becoming mentally well-adjusted people again, as well as helps them come to terms with and effectively try to repair the various negative consequences that drug abuse has brought into their lives.

Therapy

Behavioral treatment for heroin addiction can be done in an outpatient or residential setting. Again, in therapy, there are two main variations used:

Contingency management - This is a voucher-based system in which the addict will earn points with negative drug test results. These points may be exchanged for several items that promote healthy living.

Cognitive behavioral therapy - This is meant to modify the drug-related expectations and behaviors of the patient. The patient develops skills that will help them cope with the various stresses in life without them needing to turn to heroin use. Of course, this approach will be tailored individually to each user's needs.

Pharmacological Treatment (Medication)

This part of the treatment is very important since it has shown great effectiveness in reducing drug use in rehabilitating addicts, and shown greater chances of the user actually staying with the treatment program till the end in comparison with counseling and therapy alone. Pharmacological treatment has also been effective enough to show a markedly reduced risk of transmission of infectious diseases in users, as well has been effective enough to reduce criminal activity in rehabilitating or recovering addicts.

The medication used to treat heroin addiction works through the very same opioid receptors but the medications are safer and much less likely to produce harmful effects that are characteristic of addictive drugs.

The three types of medications used in treatment of heroin addiction are:

Agonists

These activate the opioid receptors.

Methadone (Dolophine® or Methadose®) is one such type of medication. As a result of being taken orally, it tends to reach the brain slowly and the impact of this is that the "high" is dampened and withdrawal symptoms are prevented from arising.

Even for patients who have been somewhat unresponsive to other forms of medications used in treating heroin addiction, many have responded well to methadone, making it a preferred treatment option since the 1960s.

This drug is only available through outpatient treatment programs that have been approved.

Partial agonists

They also activate the opioid receptors but produce a smaller response.

Buprenorphine (Subutex®) is one such drug and what it does is relieve heroin cravings without producing the "high" or other hazardous effects popular among opioids.

Suboxone® may be taken into the body either orally or sub-lingually. Besides Burenorphine, it contains naloxone – an opioid antagonist that prevents the attempt to get high by injecting the medication. When a patient decides to inject this medication, it will give rise to withdrawal symptoms which are otherwise absent when it is taken orally.

For this drug, . you need not visit specialized clinics. Burenorphine may be prescribed by certified physicians and it is also quite affordable.

Naloxone is also used in treating heroin overdoses. Taken intravenously, it has the ability to reverse the opioid-induced respiratory depression in about 2 minutes. Further treatment by the very same naloxone may be required though.

Antagonists

These block the receptors and get in the way of the "rewarding" effects of opioids.

Naltrexone (Depade® or Revia®) is one medication in this category. It is neither addictive nor a sedative and it works by blocking the action of opioids such as heroin. It may be taken either orally or as an intramuscular depot injection. Prior to taking this drug though, the patient must have been opioid free for about 7 to 10 days, otherwise it may result in withdrawal symptoms.

Vivitrol® is an intramuscular depot formulation of naltrexone and it is long-acting, so instead of getting a daily dose, all one needs is a dose administered once a month.

Support Groups

When recovering from any kind of addiction, it's critical not to overlook the value of having a good support group in place. This could be in the form of fellow recovering addicts as is the case with Narcotics Anonymous, or it could be in the form of counselors, therapists, family and friends of the recovering addict.

Chapter 6: Recovering from Heroin Addiction

With the right kind of treatment, it is possible for the addict to fully recover from dependency on the drug. However, one fact you need to be aware of is that the user should be ready to fight the urge to relapse. It is important that they receive continued support even after they are done with treatment.

Should a patient happen to relapse, it's always best to encourage them to pick themselves up and restart the road to recovery. They should never entertain the notion of giving up on recovering because in the end, they will succeed in fighting the dependency.

It is because of this fear of relapsing that there are addicts who have been sober for years and yet they still attend support group meetings and counseling every once in a while. Unfortunately, it's difficult if not impossible to entirely close the heroin chapter of one's life, and so preventative measures will need to remain in place to fight back the temptation to revert to the user's old ways.

After treatment, the patient should attempt to clean up their act and take control of their life once more. This will include mending destroyed relationships and even rebuilding people's trust in them, and it should not be assumed that it will be an easy task.

As a caregiver though, the utmost support that you can provide to the recovering addict is to allow them change for the better. Do not keep on reminding them of their follies back when they were addicted, and although it may be a good idea to keep them on close watch, do not watch them with suspicion. Allow them to adjust back into society with as much ease as possible and the chances of relapsing will be greatly reduced.

Two of the important aftercare programs a recovering addict can consider joining include 12-step group meetings, and follow-up counseling.

The more time the recovering addict spends sober, the stronger they will be to fight the urge to relapse. In the beginning, though, they should understand their triggers and stay as far away from them as they can.

People who have never suffered through addiction will find it hard, almost impossible to understand the depth of the hold the substance once had on a user's life. This point is doubly applicable to understanding the various triggers which may result in a relapse. While most people think that such a situation only need occur in cases of major stress, the truth is far from so. An addict could be tempted to return to another "hit" even if they meet people they once took heroin with, or even their former drug dealers. Psychologically, heroin addiction is strong enough to even cause temptation if recovering addicts watch movies or other media where people are taking heroin, or even if they see pictures of white powders without it *necessarily* being a scene depicting drug abuse or heroin.

Conclusion

We hope this book has helped you not only to know how to help heroin addicts before it's too late, but also to better understand the addiction itself. You know how tough heroin addiction can be. From this information, you are now able to educate other members of your family so that they can also help your loved one's recovery, and assist you in helping your loved one avoid the trap of heroin use relapse.

Often, we tend to look at heroin addicts as people who are weak, but as seen in this book, it is more an illness than an issue of willpower. The struggle among heroin addicts to overcome their addiction is genuine, and addicts should be treated gently and with patience, rather than rebuked and looked down upon.

Besides chemical and neurological changes, the addict will also tend to undergo personality changes – and it is then more than ever that they will need someone who loves them and genuinely cares for them to help with their recovery.

So be kind, have patience, and offer them your full support, and together you will be on the right track to making sure your loved one recovers from the heroin dependency, and is given a second chance to put their life back in order.

Last, I'd like to thank you for purchasing this book! If you found it helpful, I'd greatly appreciate it if you'd take a moment to leave a review on Amazon. Thanks, and Good Luck!

Made in the USA
Lexington, KY
29 June 2016